Radio Sky

BOOKS BY NORMAN DUBIE

The Horsehair Sofa (1968)
Alehouse Sonnets (1971)
Prayers of the North American Martyrs (1974)
Indian Summer (1974)
Popham of the New Song (1974)
In the Dead of the Night (1975)
The Illustrations (1977)
A Thousand Little Things (1978)
The City of the Olesha Fruit (1979)
Odalisque in White (1979)
The Everlastings (1980)
The Window in the Field (1982)
Selected and New Poems (1983)
The Springhouse (1986)
Groom Falconer (1989)
Radio Sky (1991)

W · W · NORTON & COMPANY · NEW YORK · LONDON

Radio Sky

POEMS BY Norman Dubie

Grateful acknowledgment is made to the following publications in which these poems first appeared:

The American Poetry Review: "Thomas Merton and the Winter Marsh"; "Anagram Born of Madness at Czernowitz, 23 November 1920"; "Tomb Pond"; "The Ghosts, Saratoga Springs"; "The Open Happens in the Midst of Beings"; "Looking up from Two Renaissance Paintings to the Massacre at Tiananmen Square"; "The Diatribe of the Kite"; "The Evening of the Pyramids"; "Angela."
English Language in Transition: "The Cosmological Voyages."
Kenyon Review: "Radio Sky."
Manoa: "Two Women on the Potomac Parkway"; "Homage to Philip K. Dick."
The Mississippi Review: "A Blue Hog"; "Bellevue Exchange."
New Virginia Review: "Simple Philo of Alexandria"; "In the Time of False Messiahs"; "November 23, 1989"; "Jacob Boehme Walking Outside Görlitz"; "Earth."
New England Review: "A Dream of Three Sisters"; "Inside the City Walls"; "Margaret"; "A Renunciation of the Desert Primrose"; "A Depth of Field."
Southern Review: "The Aztec Lord of the Near and Close"; "The White River Road"; "Psalm XXIII"; "Confession"; "A True Story of God"; "Revelation, 20: 11–15."

"The Aztec Lord of the Near and Close" is for Paul and Becky. "Homage to Philip K. Dick" is for Paul Cook. "A Dream of Three Sisters" is for Lois and Keri.

Gratitude is expressed to the University of Iowa Press and Bill Knott for permission to quote from his recent title *Outremer*.

A special thanks to Jeannine, Jed, and Jim Green. And the two Davids.

Copyright © 1991 by Norman Dubie
All rights reserved.
Printed in the United States of America.

The text of this book is composed in Bulmer,
with the display set in Bauer Bodoni.
Composition by PennSet, Inc.
Manufacturing by Courier Companies Inc.

First Edition

Library of Congress Cataloging in Publication Data
Dubie, Norman, 1945–
   Radio sky : poems / by Norman Dubie.
      p.   cm.
   I. Title.
PS3554.U255R3   1991
811'.54—dc20   90–44559

ISBN 0–393–02957–3

W.W. Norton & Company, Inc., 500 Fifth Avenue, New York, N. Y. 10110
W.W. Norton & Company, Ltd., 10 Coptic Street, London WC1A.1PU

1 2 3 4 5 6 7 8 9 0

For John Benedict
(1932–1990)

Contents

O N E

T W O

ONE

Brown & Dilke walked with me & back from
the Christmas pantomime.

—*John Keats*

I promise you a labyrinth, a single straight line
both invisible and infinite.

—*Jorge Luis Borges*

Radio Sky

The blue house at Mills Cross
Where the night's last firefly
Strikes its light out in a burst pod.

Under the cool stairs
You raised the chrome visor
On my aunt's old G.E.:
A faint band, green numerals
And a backlighting of amber tubes—
Each is glass, prophylactic,
With cosmic noise straight from the Swan.

Your sister,
Phyllis, had been unkind. It was hot.
Our towels floating in the tub upstairs,
We lit candles
And you poured the iced tea.

Later in bed you turned on the television
To where a station had signed off;
Making the adjustments in the contrast
We watched snow, what Phyllis said
Was literally the original light of Creation.
Genesis popping like corn in a black room. Still,
Something out of nothing. Knowing

We can't have children
You watched the flecked light
Like a rash on your stomach and breasts.
Phyllis

Is a bitch was my reply.
We made love, shared strings of rhubarb
Leached with cream. We slept
In the blue snow of the television
Drifting under the familiar worn sheet.

Thomas Merton and the Winter Marsh

I went out of the house to smoke. A thousand
Buntings in the brown stalks, scolding
The sudden cold
That's come down from Canada
That rushes the clouds to illusion, an old moon
Behind them seems to plummet—

The fat yellow spider, out earlier with the thaw,
Lowers herself on silk that
Turns solid in the cold,
Surprising us both.
She tries to climb by eating the string of ice
But can't and waits—
I put my hand under her,
Scissors over rock, she drops
Into soft hands.

I bring her inside the house
And put her in the stone cupboard
That has no ceiling, that was
A chimney in another century. If

I am ever translated into sky
I will expect my spit to turn to ice
And I will eat it and rise, unlike

The yellow spider, like the brides
And mother of Christ.

Anagram Born of Madness at Czernowitz, 23 November 1920

There are still songs to sing
On the other side of mankind.
　　　　　—Paul Celan

They were the strong nudes of a forgotten
Desert outpost, crossing through snow
Through the steam of a hot springs
Where they bathed twice daily against delirium.

It was during the conflict between the Americans
And North Koreans. We realized
They would use atomic weapons.
Our eyes were alive and you could read them.

How out on the glaciers
Angels were burning the large brooms of sunflowers,
A back growth without smoke. Each flower's head,
An alchemist's sewer plate of gold.

They were coming down in winter
And whatever they were, Mr. Ancel's ghost
Would meet them,
Saying, "You may go this far and no farther."

Like fountains in winter the heart-jet
Is bundled in shocks of straw. Now, it's cold soldiers
In a swamp cooking a skull.
The harsh glazings in my room.

Grandmother ate a sandwich while dusting
A bone cudgel
In a beam of light
In the green cellar of the museum.

When the lard factory across the street
Began burning, soap tubs collapsing with the floor,
She said, quietly,
"There, see, we must have imagined the whole thing . . .

I don't hear the bells. Do you, children?
If there's an explosion, it will come as a wind
Peppered with things—
Hold onto me and we'll sing."

Tomb Pond

—for Dave Smith

A farmer drags two lashed poles through a storm

While down the road in the snowy woods
Twelve mules are working on a tomb
For a drummer boy who was killed at Bull Run.
The farmer is wrestling two green poles.
He is building a scarecrow in the snow.
The drummer boy was his nephew. Later,

He will say that during that night
He suffered a slight stroke. It was
As if his left arm was slept upon, went numb,
And was strummed with a sensation
That did not include his thumb . . .

If there is a problem with the snow and the woods—
And, friend, there is—

Then, the destruction of an alphabet
Is the beginning of language.
It's as if some large stone
Is the cold horizon above the farmer
Erecting a scarecrow in a late-autumn storm.
The crows that watch him

Fear he has learned what they knew
All along, stealing his white corn. Alone
Too often in a room, we are open to reflection
As an old pond once built to solemnize a tomb.

Jacob Boehme Walking Outside Görlitz

—for my wife

To travel, eye-level, over the icy crossed grasses
With that cool patch of skin
Around the nipple banging like moonrise,
A red Mongol tent in the sky,
Is to find the doves moaning
Inside the haystack like summer brides.

I move in the dark of the fields
Listening to the long-running latrine
That cuts through the stinking pastures
Later to be thrashed clean
By the rocks of the river over miles . . .

I twice saw Sophia bathing in hot springs—
Pewter substituting for the white of her eyes.
She is that something that is a strong will
Willing nothing.
She is a fading utterance of mind.

I fasted for weeks

Just to see her rising from the steam, rising
Above my father's pines into light
Ground fine between the stones of a floor
And that single slow stone of the wheel.
The milled chaff was burning in her hair.

The stammering of white deer flooding the fields.

9

The Ghosts, Saratoga Springs

It's the blasts of milkweed and the sooty snow
That make the winter swamp a sorrow, that
And the offals of blood under the harsh lanterns.
A procession of iron and iron's red material:
The guns now lowered; the long, dead deer on poles.

Up in the cold lodge
An old one goes from a narrow, dark hall
Past his sickroom into the bright pantry. He is
Welcomed by the others. A door closes
Behind them, it's the color of the marsh marigold,
Shavings of a dimension out of the physical . . .

His only child was advanced, in secret; went
Ahead of him by fifty years:
That last hill, blue and dimpled, is where
They buried her. And who
Would bury a child out there? The mother,
A servant girl, was our first thought, showing
What little we knew of these aristocrats.

After the burial the poor thing
Wiped herself with a napkin twice,
Scalded it with tears and a flat iron
And served it to the mistress with lemon and a knife.
The cook is white as china, is what they said,

While at the mineral springs
The carriages in rain darken like slate: servants
In lavender filling milkcans with tonic,
With that awful sulphur of eggs.
The feedbags on the horses swelled in the rain—

Hiccups pummel the heart, and

We lost an old one in the family lodge today.
He loved too much, then not enough. He died of hiccups.
A violence to the heart. They'll bury him

Out there, on that last hill before the swamps.

A True Story of God

Henry Thoreau is lost in the Maine woods
At the center of the black pond
Standing in an Old Town canoe, his arms
Are raised welcoming a moose
Who is drunk with the methane
Of bottom grasses . . .

The moose was, in fact, already fatally shot
Through the nostril
By an Indian guide and companion
To the transcendentalist traveler
Now fainting back into his rented canoe
That is gliding toward the floundering moose—
The guide's knife

Has sliced off the upper lip of the creature
As a delicacy for his woman.
The long rubbery hairs of the lip
Will be burned away that night
At the large campfire
Where Thoreau is brooding, telling himself
That God is in nature and nature
Is in men; in that order, he thinks,
Lies the salvation of all animals
Who are placed closer to God than to humans.

Humans who, while knowing they possess a soul,
Become useless. Useless and cruel. Thoreau jumps,
The fat of the lip
Snapping from the flames like gunfire.

Revelation, 20: 11–15

—for Tito

He was a farmboy who had drowned that Wednesday
While trying to swim two gray horses across the river.
We had met him once at the cemetery
Where our father was burying his aunt.
We had watched with him while two limousines, a pickup,
And a cab from Bath entered the gate. He looked
At the urn of African violets and then with his shoulder
Tipped it, riling some yellow slag-burning bees.
He laughed and ran past the trees toward the beach
And the wildness of his arms and legs
Made me think he might be climbing a tall building.
But he was running away; slowing in the dunes,
He was still in sight even as we were dragged
To our mother by the enraged deacon Blaisdale.
He said we were common vandals.
You were silent. I said
That little shit Smithy had done it.
We began crying. Miss Rose, who had witnessed everything,
Crossed the lawn to save us from judgment.
Deacon Blaisdale began apologizing, our mother
Interrupted him with what would happen
If ever again he laid hands on either of us—
By now the Smith boy jumping into the Atlantic—
In my heart I thanked him for bringing
Down the righteous six-foot deacon
Who was going very red in the face as our own mother
Slapped me for calling the dead boy a name.
Well, he wasn't dead yet, but when he was
We were amazed.

The Open Happens in the Midst of Beings

—Martin Heidegger

The coroner said a white picket fence,
Passed in a split second,
Will induce a fit in an epileptic . . .
It was a yellow Jaguar
With a black steamer trunk
Strapped to the rack. He wet himself,
Straightened against the accelerator,
And entered Smith's barn at 90 mph—

He bit through his tongue was all,
Left one cow senseless
But with a sweeter milk. And
A young sow miscarried like a trout,
Just a plug of mucous and suds at the mouth.

You laughed. His wife
Passed the cake. Down at the dock
Two waiters, clearly in love,
Smoked while speaking
To the rocks and lake.

The trees were frantic.

We walked through pasture,
Along the river, so not to be late.
But stopped at the pin oak
Where you stepped out of your skirt
And into a haze of gnats;
By the time they passed, you were
On your back in the water.

Leaf shadow draped over you
From the waist to the feet . . .

We were asked not to be late.
At dinner the psychic's assistant
Without permission
Took some straw from your hair.
You blushed. I gave her boss
A look that cost him his concentration.
Still, he told your mother
Her license plate number. I frowned
Through the applause, pushing
Olives around with a spoon.
He then hypnotized our red-haired waitress
And a moth flew out of her mouth.

It brought me back to the pin oak
Where, in the midst of beings
Who were weeping, we laughed and swam
Not quite like the undoubted trout
Who were beside themselves
On the riverbed in a cold white spout. . . .

The White River Road

It was that confusion of flu
With birches and sumac flying past
The bus window. I remembered a passage
From Pasternak. How a quick movement
Of blue made a conquest of the pines and grass.
There, on the stump dais at Peredelkino,
He saw the winter maze of birches
Turn into a violent sea
Vomiting a hundred thousand red shrimp
Onto a desolate cold beach. And
It was nausea I was feeling
While the Greyhound made its way
Through the wet hollow of Williamstown, Vermont.
A country road surveyed by cows.
The bus driver drank
From his black-and-red chequered thermos.
I ached. Sweat soaking my shirt,
And then pines with a sun
Setting behind them
Gave a pulse to my stomach
That had turned as we passed a small farmhouse.

At the depot
You put your cool hand to my forehead
And said there was potato soup and new bread waiting.
I frowned, going green under the dome light.
By morning I was weak but fine, first snow
Outside. You stepped from the tub
And sat backward in the cane chair,
Your hair wet and stringy; you said
The flaring lines of your hips and breasts
Were now outrageous— I thought, No,

16

A violin of flesh with a blond tuft
For a chin rest, hands dipped in albumen,
A tinny resonance of wind
And the water faucets banging out in the sheds
Were made of a happy calamitous aluminum
That could wake the dead.

A Depth of Field

—for David St. John

The trailer, a bubble of aluminum and glass,
One hundred of them in a field
Beside the poplars and the frozen lake—
Everywhere else tennis courts, some
With the nets still there, the posted
Snow fences of another place, wind and heavy ice
In general for miles . . .

It's there, in the weather, my father chews his cigar
At the old scriveners bench,
A first-year medical student in my mother's apron
Dissecting a black cat, daubing
At the wide trench.

I look down through the curb of the skylight
And see it all, the whole sum
Of a winter landscape sucked into the open cat
Like a red sock into the vacuum.

When you faint there *is* a sudden tunneling.
There is also the smell
Of smoke and formaldehyde on your father's shirt.
And while you wake, for that instant,
There are white monkeys at all the gates.

The Aztec Lord of the Near and Close

The prince was buried in a squatting position
Suspended in a net from the rafter pole
That was made of ironwood
And cut through the center of a huge brick capstone.
In the mouth of the slain prince there were pebbles
Of obsidian. His thumbs
Were buried in the floor beneath him
To keep him from the cleverness of the dead.
The eyes of a yellow dog
Were placed with his thumbs as compensation.

Two palms made of gold
With two rootballs of jade were planted in the burial shaft,
And the prince
Hovered just above them. The site for the burial
Was a mesquite grove. The prince
Crossed over to the other world
Disguised as an oriole, and while the sun set
He was welcomed by women who had died in childbirth.
They wore gowns of chili-red cotton.

Because the prince had a strong young heart
They made him the god of weddings
Which he visits bedizened in wing feathers—hawk,
Macaw, and parrot.
His name became *Thalocan*.
He attends all marriages within the eight deserts.
Just to say his name is sufficient blessing
For all the days of your life. But it is said
That if you know the secrets of his burial
Then you will have a blessing of nights.
Nights like the blue underbelly of a lizard

Slowly sinking in a cool lake, fat orange carp
Rising around him so the sun will never be late.

Looking up from Two Renaissance Paintings to the Massacre at Tiananmen Square

Fruit flies lift off the bowl of brown pears.
The volume of the television is turned down.

If you watch Christ raise Lazarus from the dead
You will observe that he is always
Upwind of him. The unfortunate
Sisters are downwind
With bags of cloves pushed to their faces.
Olive trees, on the dry hillside, lean
In these famous paintings, leaving the direction
Of the wind not in question.
Christ, if you believe the Italians,
Was like most magicians—

Clean and well positioned.
It's summer, supper is finished
Except for its odors. Before dusk begins
There's an hour of strong light
Which would never offend the religious.
It's in this light
That I look up at the bleached screen.
There, in the silence, students fall before machines.
It's as if they are the faint
Of a mass healing. In a suburb of the city
There is a mound of bodies which will be burned.

In Tehran, if death is a woman, then her hem
Will drag over the ground. But death
Is that bearded man dressed in a black gown.

Confession

The General's men sit at the door. Her eyes
Are fat with belladonna. She's naked
Except for the small painted turtles
That are drinking a flammable cloud
Of rum and milk from her navel.

The ships out in the harbor
Are loosely allied
Like casks floating in bilge.
The occasional light on a ship
Winks. In the empty room of the manuscript
Someone is grooming you
For the long entrance into the dark city.

They'll hang the General.

Then with torches they'll search for his children.
Men and women
Are seen jumping from the burning hotel.
Journalists, in no hurry,
Elect to take the elevator. They walk
Out of the building, stepping over corpses . . .
You are listening to loud bells.

The corpses get up and follow the journalists.
It's unfair that while rehearsing
For death they actually succumbed to it.
But no one sobs.
Shirts and dresses billowing as they fall.
Something inhuman in you watched it all.
And whatever it is that watches,
It has kept you from loneliness like a mob.

The Diatribe of the Kite

They come from the white barrier of noon
Where two forces of magnetism, one weak
And one strong, combine
To create a cruel sea of iron filings
Over which, as unlikely pilgrims, they journey.

As our sun rises, and they sleep,
Only then do they become
The ancestors of whom we are ashamed.

These two behemoths, one red and one green,
Sulk over willow sticks, rice paper,
And a wooden pot of glue. There is gold leaf
Like raked fire between them.

They swallow blood with milk. They feast
On the roasted tongue of prisoner angels.

When they nap, in the late afternoon,
The earth moves. . . . They wake
Like simple accordians. And they are doomed.
Much of what they know, they learned
While grazing in the field with animals.

Their kite will be flown in a storm. It is
The crossed sticks of punishment
Above the city
Of their making. In time, they have taken

Two names: *Yang Baibing, Deng Xiaoping.*
In rhyme, they are joyously insane.
They are the immortality of the nursery

Where they reign—
Those ancestors for whom we are ashamed.

The Evening of the Pyramids

A summer night in the desert is as welcome
As the savant in robes
Who's come to build an aqueduct of stone.
Here, the night will not support ghosts.
They visit at noon
And at the poles of twilight.
The red caftans of the angry horsemen
Float on the distant skyline

Where date palms are blistered gold. The birds
Who eat from these trees
Mistake the air for alcohol. In a hot wind
The dusty postal road is lined with palms,
Their dried fruit, a storm of castanets.
And then suddenly there's silence. . . .

The Sphinx was to the backs of the Frenchmen
Deployed in squares: at the centers
Napoleon placed large cannon, donkeys
Loaded with provisions,
And two hundred scholars he found
In a heavy winter conscription.
A single lengthening report of rifle fire
Left six thousand Mameluke horses
Dying on their sides like fish.
The Mameluke men were stripped, emptied into the Nile.
The smell of gunpowder
Wafted into the slums of Cairo.

The next evening, Bonaparte
In the Pyramid of Cheops asked to be left
In the King's Chamber, empty

But for the sarcophagus of granite
Cut at the original site of Atlantis.

When Napoleon left the tomb
For daylight, he was visibly changed
But would say nothing of what he'd seen.
The very same room had shaken
Both Alexander and Caesar.
Even when dying, at Elba, he persisted
In repeating, "You would not have believed it.
Is it evening?"

The Emperor said nothing.
What he saw can be reported faithfully,
And its significance is plain—
There was a dark room and an empty coffer for a king.

TWO

And when our oxygen

Thins to a pin who cares Who's x Who's y—
That altered acme stares at me—icily—
That game where time (come to theme) recombines
To dial them new stars night never fell on:

It beads up as my eye, friend planet.

—Bill Knott

A Dream of Three Sisters

From night rocks, above an ocean alive with yellow kelp,
The ghost of Samuel Taylor Coleridge tossed
Raw chunks of a disquieting muse
To three ragged mermaids . . . each
Had a long tooth the white of gruel.
Coleridge knelt in his velvet coat
With a prune-dark dog
That barked at the sagging breasts of the women.
When the sisters stopped tearing at their meat
To scowl back at the benefactor, the dog
Would whimper under the silks of a tent
In which he and Coleridge slept
Like evangelists of a new forebearance.
Two old philosophers not troubled by death
Like the moon Phobos, which rises and sets
Twice each day above this martian landscape.
Here, the ghost of Coleridge sat, fully disconsolate,
With little more than thought for the fatal opiate . . .
But how, you must ask, exactly did that dog
Become spirit? It was a winter day
On a small farm in Massachusetts.
White-winged horses were feeding like geese
From the very bottom of a pond placed among trees.
The dog was to be shot that morning by the farmer Smith
Who shot himself instead. His wife
Drowned the mongrel the next day
In a sack filled with nails for weight.
The dog was not sick. It was rumored
He had killed the cat. It was in this manner
That a mongrel entered the esteemed company
Of the addict Coleridge.
The afterlives of the gentle farmer and cat

29

Are an open subject. Perhaps
They live on the happy side of the same ocean
That is a torment to the dog and poet.
They were the first to burst upon this lonely sea.
They often wonder what it must be like
Being wholly ordinary.

Homage to Philip K. Dick

The illegal ditch riders of the previous night
Will deliver ice today.
The barbers up in the trees are Chinese.
They climb with bright cleats, bearing machetes—
It's a season
Of low self-esteem for date palms on the street.

My visitor was at the door yesterday.
In a blue sere of a sucker suit.
An *I Like Ike* button
On the lapel. Holding a cup of sawdust.
He breathed through his eyes, crusted
With pollen.

I was not confused. It was God
Come to straighten my thoughts.
Whole celestial vacuums
In the trunk of his pink Studebaker.
He would smoke and cough.
I sat very still, almost at peace with myself.

He had shot a deer in the mountains. He thought
Last year's winter kill was worse than usual.
I told him I didn't know about guns.
Something forming on his forehead—a gloriole
Of splattered sun over snow.
We drank our lemonade in silence.

He asked if he could go. He joked
About his wife's tuna casserole. As a gift
I signed for him my last paperback.
He left the book of matches. I'll not enroll

In the correspondence course it offers
For commercial artists. What a relief

That the barbers in the trees are Chinese.
Green fronds are dropping in twos and threes
Around the bungalow, lessons
In the etiquette of diseased parrots. Bill Cody
Said it first, "If there is no God, then I am
His prophet." Stop it. Please stop it.

Inside the City Walls

A small boy in shock with a blue popsicle
In the dark hallway of a Montreal hospital—
His mother floats past me
Away from the nurses' station,
Her dead husband's silver glasses in her hand
Exactly as I had learned to hold the javelin:
The first position,
Arm trailing while the wrist turns,
Thumb in rebellion, the whole body
Mindless of its gathering speed, head lolling
Impossibly, the spear
Is pulled from the chest
Where the foot is first firmly planted . . .

The Bus Stopped in Fields of Misdemeanor

—for Brittony

I don't know why they turn the irrigation
On the oranges before they are frozen.
And you are not my daughter, but my daughter's friend.
Your mother is dead in Los Angeles.
Charles Dickens, dying,
Dreamt of large work horses
With flaring tinctured gums
Charging down a mountain of fine white powders . . .
It meant nothing to him. It was a blessing.

Forgive me, in the middle of all this,
If I ask your pardon. The newspapers
Report an icy canker in the orchards.
The growers are alarmed but optimistic.

It is a winter morning in the desert. I woke
To one of those heavy trains of language:
It's Hannah's friend, Brittony, her mother's dead
From an overdose of heroin.
I honestly don't know why
It bothered me so much, it's almost out of season
And I am of the enemy. And we are legion.

Two Women on the Potomac Parkway

On Tuesday's bus I heard the man from State
Describe for his mistress
How soldiers in Ethiopia
Raped an eleven-year-old shepherdess . . .
Muriel, I swear he thought
It would turn her on. I told Sam
She probably *did* shred paper with the best of them.

We saw that photograph on television.
It looked like Reptile Man
Dressed in enema bags. You know
The other one with two men in leather jackets—
It reminded Sam of the boy in Maine
Who rode his motorcycle along our pines
And into a black half-acre hatch of mayflies.
The bike dragged him down the mountain highway,
A thousand bugs
Like live soot in his mouth and nostrils.
It made Sam sad. He thought Mapplethorpe
Was gifted. Two of our children
Dead in as many years.

Look how the snow has drifted
Up to the slats on that fence. It's like the dirty
French postcards you buy in museums now.
The snow is brazen.
Mr. Lincoln sitting there above it all.
Mr. Lincoln's Tad, who suffered a cleft palate,
Died not long after his father was martyred.

From Tuesday's bus I saw three congressmen
In fur coats. They were waiting for the light to change.
The fat one's hat blew off,
His cronies laughing at him. Doubled over
He began to wade across the lawns; finally
Up to his waist in drifts, just half a man
Dressed in animal skins, he reached
Into that vast pornography of snow
And rescued his hat and honor. It wasn't funny, Muriel.
It made me sick, if you must know.

The Cosmological Voyages

—in memory of Ian Fletcher

The sillies of this desert village
Were roasting lambs beside the well.
You and the boy
Who trained in tanks at Sandhurst
Circling the skull of a camel.
Ants as a kind of language
Streaming from the sinus cavity of the animal.

The surgeon called you back to the train.
He framed a telegram from Montgomery
And another from General Smuts. He had
You inoculated for typhus twice over Christmas.
The fever sent you a dream
Of a dead secretary of the Afrika Korps:
Her torn green dress, and the broken
Trestle table with a short leg
Made equal by a paper edition of Byron.
Her white finger on the telegraph key
Produced the loud chattering of human teeth.

An old friend had pasted on a camera lens
The scales of a translucent fish
Netted in the cold sea off Crete. The new petals
For the shutter cut from balsa.
It stands, he said,
That the devil answers even in engines:
Yards of salt hay burning in a December whirlwind,
And London blacked out . . .

The *Bismarck* is near the coast of Finland
And the fallen night bomber

Photographed for the *Daily Sketch*
Is better than a Sargent—
Haphazard, foreshortened, and swept.
The photographer
Was a young Czech sheltered in the suburbs.
He suffered from corns
And made a plaster of spruce gum
For them. You drank Christmas sherry
With him the same evening
Your boat left for East Africa. The way
The black tea from Burma was tucked
Into your shirt. He wished
You a safe passage. The stars
That night over the water

Were a pure doggerel spoken by the hollow
Of a skull—that ferocious original camel
Whose winter burden
Was an old magus traveling from Algeria.

Psalm XXIII

It was the first Wednesday of a scarcity of candles.
The planes, of course, came in waves. They came
With the dinner bell. Only Eric
Remained upstairs. Inside the orange room
Plaster settled on everyone and in the soup.
Outside snow fell
Heavily around our houses. In the garden
The broken water pipes gushed and froze
Over a horse whose backside was crushed by fallen bricks;
The heated water hissed and as the horse
Took on ice, still propped up with its forelegs,
It stood like a feeding mantis, the awful mouth
Open around its swollen tongue.
We dipped our napkins in the thin soup
And, draping them over our faces, walked
Out into the smoke. The munitions factory
On the hillside blossomed and burned. It was ear-splitting,
And sudden. I got sick.
In shame, I went back inside, changing into father's pajamas.
Uncle shot the horse; it shattered,
A fallen chandelier with all its candles white,
Save one red tier.
Eric remained upstairs, more out of disgust
Than fear.
We had a car, and had hoarded petrol.
In the morning
We would drive to the Swedish Legation.
Mother said that on a burnt-out building,
With chalk, someone wrote: *Lily, the Aunt was killed.*
I have room now I think
For both you and the children. Where are you?
When there's snow on the ground

The automobiles, lorries, and trains are very plain to see
And the bombers have a field day.
Men pass mornings scattering ashes
Around the factories and in Soldiers' Cemetery
Where the Americans bomb mercilessly. Out in the garden
The homeless cut great steaks from the sides
Of Uncle's dead horse.
Uncle thought this both practical and wholesome.
But when they dragged out its intestines
He shot above their heads and cursed them.
They ran in the direction of the park.
Father wanted to know if there was anything
Eric wanted. He said that to start with
He'd drop a bomb on that horse's carcass
And have it done with. . . .
Father said everyone was nervous
And Eric could go to his room until breakfast.
I saw him once again
That evening in a coffin.

A Renunciation of the Desert Primrose

—for J. Robert Oppenheimer

I am tired of the black-and-white photograph
Of a government bunkhouse, tin and pine,
And the orchids in the catalpa trees
Shriveled to twine. A white birdcage
Hangs from a rafter.
This was the sleep of mathematics, the poor facts
Of primrose. An MP struts
With a large sack filled with rattlesnakes.
The tar-paper windmill kneels out in the dunes,
Battered hat of the Pilgrims.
Beside the bunkhouse,
A tower and checkpoint. Again, a large sack
Slack with mind. The head of the Medusa inside.
Across the dunes
Dead flowers scatter like X rays of the thorax.
I have fallen behind. . . .

Angela

A bottle of mineral water from Montreal
With an olive at the bottom.
The box of chocolates
Faded to the green of pondwater.
Because it was spring, winter remained
Only in the sunken back of the white gelding—
There and under the blue spruce
Which ran to the ridgepole.
She moved with the great weight
And perfume of the lilac blossoms
That were her background
In this little miracle of childhood
That is dotage.

Dragging a bucket of coal to the shed,
She stops to spit at a squirrel;
Somewhere across the river, she knows
A man is confessing petty crimes
To his mistress. How disgusting, she thinks,
Hurling lumps of coal at the red squirrel.

X had died. Y had died.
She was just

Older now under the gray skies. Yet, last night,
In the prehistory of her spirit,
She leapt at the burning curtains—
She leapt, a happy organization of bones
Wired like a pterodactyl
Before an orange-and-red watercolor of sunrise.

A Blue Hog

I didn't have to buy the acid.
I found it in an old battery in the barn
Where the cows make sea noises
And the cobwebs are plated gold.
There were packets of birdseed, white floats
Of cork, turpentine, and an old black fishline
Which shouldn't have worked but did.
All of it a sin for the taking—
I chose the acid for its smoke
And the fishline to tie around my toe
To remind me of the smoke.
I threw the rotten apples into the yard
And the blue hog charged.
He was unpardonable, having
Killed my sister's child. John couldn't
Butcher him—*to eat that hog*
Would be to eat the child.
I poured the acid into pink Christmas bulbs
And sewed them into the hollowed apples.
I put them out into the sun to soften.
The hog swallowed them whole like smoke.
By the time he looked under himself
He was already broke. My long dress shook.
He stopped to give me a look,
And then ran straight at the barn.
His head and shoulders passed through the boards.
The horse inside
Had a hissing fit over him. Nobody
Has ridden that horse since
Except for the devil
Who's said to still be in the district.

Margaret

I'm a frogman, she said. Naked by the water
Under a lean of canvas she'd sewn
With a thick paraffin thread.
She gestured. When we pulled him
From the river
His left leg was meal. Crayfish in the hair.
The riverbottom left his shoulder
Layered and crocheted—
My sister's pearl knitting needles
Clicking in my head. I told
The sheriff I wouldn't do it again.

I knew him once. His Chevy threw a rod.
I made it with him
On the hood of the old truck.
It was out at the dump beyond Yuma.
It felt like I had bread crumbs
All over my mouth. Wacky with the sun,
I sure did it with him enough
That afternoon. I didn't

Know it was him who'd drowned.
They said it was his cousin.
He had a three-cornered scar
At the small of his back. And a deposit
Of calcium on the tailbone.
We're not much, you know?

He was tangled in yellow tree roots,
He spun in the currents,
A fishhook and line running
From his thumb.
A whole new ball of wax, I thought.

I wanted to be an astronaut.
But failed the mathematics
Twice in one summer.
So I raise Nubian goats.
My favorite has a purple manure
That comes out like steaming packets
Of tobacco mulch. He sprays
The shack with his seed—
It hasn't needed paint in three years.

I just took my shorts off
When you two came down the hill.
It's that rubber suit I wear
When I dive into the chute and cave.
Sometimes I just feel
Like old air in a patched tire. Then,
I get my Seagrams and come out here.
You two look married. Not that I care.
You wouldn't believe what I was just thinking—
Your husband's the only living man
Left in this county
Who knows that I bleach my hair.

Bellevue Exchange

The ground on which the ball bounces
Is another bouncing ball.
—Delmore Schwartz

A large man rowing in a white tub
While the fog sweeps over him
And the orange pines of the island
Reflect everywhere in the brightly tiled room.
The red shell of the razor clam
And a cup of soap rest on a fresh towel.

He lowers his head, moose moving like his genitals
Through the room, he steps out onto the water—
He hears the telegraph of glass beads, the decades
Of drowned nuns traveling to Quebec. Now
A yellow rain like straw piercing the lake.
A long narrow waist in conflict

With large breasts and hips, she crosses
The room with both hands on the full glass
Of bourbon. He reaches through the fog for it,
And a bell from land
Cancels everything. Towels tossed
To the floor. The water climbing for him.

46

Simple Philo of Alexandria

You will see what is behind me
But my face will not be seen by you.
—Exodus 33:23

For what are we to think? But that Philo
Goaded his rich merchant brother Lysimachus
Into selling winecasks, jewels,
And all his servants
To finance a projectile to the moon.

Philo's friends, brothers in the dark prospect,
Gathered with the Emperor's mistresses
Just below Nero's courtyard
Where the red rocket wrapped in straw
Sat in its brass caution of gunpowder.

With burning cane Philo ignites
The fuse, which is a braid of human hair.
The rocket climbs like a goose
Breaking out of the water, flying
Through the fire of outbank ether.

It veers into the carts of Charlemagne
And having lost its course, passes our moon—
A seer of Nero's watches the projectile
Cross the orbits of planets,
Through a storm of chalk and bones,
Passing out of the Cosmos . . .

Now eternal in its voyage,
It blazes away from the venue of the seer,
Which was thought to be nearly absolute.
It does not return to its Emperor, burning

Most of Rome.
It keeps on going—insubstantial, a spirit vehicle,

It begins to compose itself,
For the very first time, inside the mind of Philo
Who is one soul
Among the incalculable number of souls,
All as inseparable
From simple Philo as from the whole.

November 23, 1989

—after Blake

Two rising flukes of green water
Joined and fell like marble
On the black ships which tipped
And sunk. A gull was thrown against the sky.
The cloaked men and women on the cliff
Watched the clouds in darker battery
Move against the very ground of sea.
The water is a turning page of scripture
Pleased with the impossible needs
Of pilgrims who stood arranged in disbelief.

It is the Thursday of a certain need
That must yet become more desperate
If wilderness is to be raised above itself
Like fire in the airshafts of a skyscraper.

What if in some long thanksgiving
They refused as friends to be ordinary company
And instead thought of themselves
As the eventual dead.
Then, the wattle fence made to limit geese
Would collapse and become the skids of memory
Gone beyond Babylon
Into crowded streets where hooves
Of horses sparked with simple symmetry
Like those biggest bones that by necessity
Must bear away the most meat.

In the Time of False Messiahs

—circa 1648

He sat in the shade of trees at moonrise
Following with his eyes the tracks of fleas
Who were hunting wolves. A poor rabbi
Dressed in a paper gown, he ate a black potato.
Women danced behind him like the snow.
There were boats in the sky above him
And they were lowering ropes.
There was famine everywhere in Poland.

The fires of the city made him cold
So he walked into the forest.
He walked along a brook into the hills.
He praised the white trees
And the owls that nested in them:
Their simple fires of digestion, the bones
Of mice igniting in their bowels.
He reached up and grasped a rope.
He climbed into the boat.
There was famine everywhere in Poland.

Everywhere below him there was hope.

50

Earth

—for James Green

It is never enough. The obese flagellants in their cells
Stand like cows
On the night before the birth of Christ,
The tail's hard burr of manure
Swatting sour desert flies, the stalls
Heavy with boughs of cedar, mounds of salt—
The cows shout hallelujah at the night.

The night itself is a passage of vaulting milk,
A long innuendo of crows in flight
Across a dark rainbow. Geronimo
And the loud noise of winter thunder say so . . .

A black death once lodged in the flesh like oranges:
It became a triumph of smoke, now just body sacks
Falling slowly into a river.
In the underground baths, hot rouged asses
Of men and women bounce
Like rising beads of water from the river
Separated briefly from itself on an unlikely trampoline
Of mass burial by water. Time is its simple motor.
That is the truth about the river.

But it is never enough. So the cows
Stand like applause, which is the sound of running water
Before the miracle that is not enough.
It was night that made explorers of us—
Into it, with some old air left in the lungs,
We plunge; millions more
Of us than we know, down the river
And out of the mouth

Into a moment both oceanic and subtle. We hoped
It was all ours,
And like Apaches, we made our last language of smoke.

A Physical Moon Beyond Paterson

—for Brian

William Carlos Williams had finished
His mid-December rounds
In an old hospital made of field stones.
He walked out into the late-afternoon sun
And sat in his car, an emerald Hudson.
He said *no* twice and straightened,
The car slowly going down the rural hill.
He saw a row of technicians dressed in lead coats
And yesterday's baby with a bowel obstruction.
All of the previous night
This road was plowed. The snow
Climbing six feet now on either side.
With little warning a hot spike
Had entered his elbow. He had suffered a stroke.
Maybe he was lost for oxygen, some odd gaiety
Overwhelmed him while descending a winter hill.
He began to play the green Hudson
Violently against the two walls of snow
Leaving the seasonal paint of the car
On a quarter mile of water turned crystal.
Accelerating, he shot across the state highway
Coming to rest in a marsh with a deep brook.
He was crying and singing, awake
With the spongy earth below him.
He was not the Polish woman of his night-calls:
She endured two hours of labor
Scouring her kitchen floor. She curtsied
And froze, delivering in that position
A seven-pound girl.
And that's the glory. For a moment
This old man was a rough sluice of toboggan

Gone tobogganing.
And then he just walked out across
The colossal toxic wilderness of New Jersey,
The holiest dish to whiteness passing over. . . .

NORMAN DUBIE was born in Barre, Vermont, in April 1945. His poems have appeared in many magazines, including *Antaeus*, *The Paris Review*, *The New Yorker*, *The American Poetry Review*, *Kenyon Review*, *Southern Review*, and *Poetry*. He has won the Bess Hokin Award of the Modern Poetry Association and fellowships from the National Endowment for the Arts, The Ingram Merrill Foundation, and The John Simon Guggenheim Memorial Foundation. He lives in Tempe, Arizona, with his wife, Jeannine, and his daughter, Hannah. Mr. Dubie is a teacher at Arizona State University.